I0867515

The Blue Bridge

Also By Maurya Simon

La Sirena: A Novella in Verse
The Wilderness: New & Selected Poems, 1980-2016
The Raindrop's Gospel: The Trials of St. Jerome & St. Paula
Cartographies: Uncollected Poems, 1980-2005
WEAVERS
Ghost Orchid
A Brief History of Punctuation
The Golden Labyrinth
Speaking in Tongues
Days of Awe
The Enchanted Room

The Blue Bridge

Maurya Simon

Etruscan Press

© 2024 by Maurya Simon
All rights reserved. Except for brief quotations in critical articles or reviews,
no part of this book may be reproduced in any manner without prior written permission from the publisher:

Etruscan Press
Wilkes University
84 West South Street
Wilkes-Barre, PA 18766
(570) 408-4546

Wilkes University

www.etruscanpress.org

Published 2026 by Etruscan Press
Printed in the United States of America
Cover art: *Light Keepers*, 2014 © Andrea Kowch
Cover design by Jess Morandi
Interior design and typesetting by Kari Bayait
The text of this book is set in Minion Pro.

First Edition

17 18 19 20 5 4 3 2 1

Library of Congress Cataloguing-in-Publication Data

Names: Simon, Maurya, 1950- author
Title: The blue bridge / Maurya Simon.
Other titles: Blue bridge (Compilation)
Description: First edition. | Wilkes Barre, PA : Etruscan Press, 2025. |
Summary: "Maurya Simon's twelfth volume of poems, The Blue Bridge, is a literary tour de force that bears witness to the twenty-first century's dire and lasting dangers brought about by human folly and greed. At the same time that it laments species loss, it honors the enduring lives of small creatures, and the perseverance and adaptability of larger animals. Simon also charts the journey of her own life in an America that is increasingly marked by violence and division, as well as by the ameliorating and lasting ties between people. At turns philosophical, playful, irreverent, and passionate, this book showcases a poet's work at the peak of her powers, as she illuminates how the bonds between spirit and flesh, and each other, sustain us"-- Provided by publisher.
Identifiers: LCCN 2025048719 | ISBN 9798990767829 paperback acid-free paper

Subjects: LCGFT: Poetry
Classification: LCC PS3569.I4827 B58 2026
LC record available at https://lccn.loc.gov/2025048719
Please turn to the back of this book for a list of the sustaining funders of Etruscan Press.

This book is printed on recycled, acid-free paper.

"An awake heart is like a sky
that pours light."

—Hafiz

For Robert, again and again

CONTENTS

Acknowledgements

I'm grateful to the editors of the following literary magazines and journals who first published these poems in their periodicals' pages, sometimes in slightly altered versions:

February Reverie: *The Southern Review*
Desert Tortoise Lament: *Red Canary Magazine*
Indonesian Corpse Flower: *Literary Matters*
A Hive Mind: *Beltway Poetry Quarterly*
In the Mohave: *Paintbrush Magazine* (Calif. Native Plant Society)
Omnicide: *Poetry* and *Columbia Granger's World of Poetry*
Landscape in December: *Red Canary Magazine*
Transformations: *Image: A Journal of the Arts and Religion*
Gone: *Literary Matters*
Magic Bullets: A Meditation on Loss: *The Hudson Review*
Unfinished Poem: *Cream City Review*
Pain Log #1: *Michigan Quarterly Review*
Pain Log #2: *Michigan Quarterly Review*
Spindrift: *Beltway Poetry Quarterly*
A Lament for My Elders: *Ploughshares*
Saturday Night Fever: *New Letters*
Quotation Marks: A Bestiary: *The Hudson Review*
A Theory of Eyebrows: *Smartish Pace*
The Slash: *The Hudson Review*
Sheelah-Na-Gig: *The Manhattanville Review*
@: A Triptych: *The Southern Review*
Untold Lives of Ancient Greece: *The Hudson Review*
Rules of Thumb: *Beltway Poetry Quarterly*
The Blue Bridge: *The Southern Review*
On Some Hand-Me-Downs from G-d: *American Literary Review*
Creation Redux: *New Letters*
The Widow: *Beltway Poetry Quarterly*
An Accounting of His Life: *The Hudson Review*
Requiem: *New Letters*

A Hive Mind

Civilization exists by geological consent,
subject to change without notice.

—Will Durant

Omnicide

And when our children ask,
Why did you do nothing as the world
was dying? What will we tell them?

Will we say, *We didn't know how*
sick it was, or admit, *We gathered all*
our rosebuds while we could,

Old Time was still a-flying—?
It's now the end of everything,
our children will say, *go crawl*

into your arks and sail off destitute into
your doom, and leave us only
our shadows. And our kids

will light candles across seven continents
empty now of lions, kangaroos, ravens,
pelicans, dromedaries, squirrels—

devoid of praying mantises, koalas, ants,
cobras, snails, Doberman Pinschers, pigs,
vultures, lizards, and alley cats.

Our little ones will hide in caves with blind
cockroaches, together feeding on the algae
glowing in neon greens and blues

across dolomite and limestone walls.
They'll leave no pictographs behind,
no sprayed handprints, no artful gods.

Such silence now, they'll say, *this you've*
bequeathed us, this human indifference.
And we'll beg them, *Survive.*

Desert Tortoise Lament

Long down the shadow-heavy hedgerows,
I watch the hare hurrying to ensnare his glory,
while I plod on with patience and without worry,
my scaled feet pigeon-toed, my belly raking furrows.

I'll live my century thinking my slow thoughts.
My tongue, thick as an obstinate root, works well
to teach sparrows which grubs to pluck from gravel.
My leathery gaze stops centipedes dead in their tracks.

Years ago, the Tongva carried my tender carapace
across a flooded desert to save and honor their sister;
later, I wandered delirious, searching for a history
that would guide me back to my people's place.

But a man filled with music found me, who, unwary,
harmonized with a hope beyond himself—rescued me
from stone-throwing boys and chained dogs gone crazy
with neglect, and from a mowing machine. Near an aviary

I live now as a suburbanite, a slow talisman for a race
in which my stride gets pitted against a rabbit's hop.
I always win. A sickle moon grins at me where I stop,
my old heart languorous, my past nearly erased.

Odd Winter

(Southern California, 2022)

February & the magnolias turn wildly flamboyant.
Cherry, pear, & tangelo trees blossom deliriously.

Balmy days, balmy nights as stars drift off in darkness
towards the Milky Way's spirals of snowdrops & ice.

Far from predatory black holes, hurtling meteorites, &
the fourth dimension's seductions, something's wrong:

here in the West the rain's missing in action; a fleet
of avid mosquitos shadows me as I walk to the P.O.—

What strange winter god has cursed us, when snakes
forsake hibernation for the off chance of catching

a mousey snack, when house wrens, months early,
build delicate & messy nests in empty flower pots?

Their chicks may get heat stroke, or turn hard boiled
and never hatch. Let's gather our tribes and begin

devising how to survive on these parched lands,
while kindred creatures curse us—until they can't.

Indonesian Corpse Flower

As a Juggernaut of Blooms,
this Amorphophallus looms above
the Huntington Gardens' crowds,
an equatorial cloud of putrid odor
spilling over the heads of its viewers.
We mill around its towering spadix,
clicking furiously on mobile phones.
What a marvel at this despairing time:
hourly traffic jams to see this spathe
unfurl like the beginning of the world.

A Hive Mind

Somewhere safe is the honeyed center
of the maze, where yellow echoes vibrate
their wings and a family of atoms
clusters itself into a sanctuary.

Some days the mind buzzes with joy,
as if hearing something good
is enough, even if it's just the hymn
of a willow breathing,

or a neighbor speaking in Pashto,
or the clamor of hail.
Maybe it's only in prayer that we
tune in to God's isolate mind,

feeling our bones straining towards
its waggle dance. Let's calibrate
our collective spirit to the key of
green, to mind-sync our planet love.

Hippocampus Histrix

Little sea dragon,
with your prehensile tail
looped around slender strands
of eelgrass,

how delicate the fluttering
of your tiny fins,
your eyes luminous
as sequins.

I salute your long snout—
a white-striped bugle—
and your brood pouch
quite distended

with eggs so deftly
deposited
by a lady seahorse
as vulnerable as you are.

She's quietly fled
these inshore
sea grasses where
shrimp trawlers trample

your breeding-feeding
grounds, but still
you calmly siphon plankton
into your snout,
then later unpocket
your brood of pups, expelling
them into an ocean world,
wondrous and savage.

A Pastoral

Dictator Idi Amin's 100-room wildlife lodge,
scattered along Uganda's White Nile, is now a ruin
housing wart hog families sheltering in its kitchens,
as well as armored pangolins and porcupines who scout
out mossy bedrooms and crumbling verandas. Occasionally,
smirking jackals, leopards, and red-assed baboons prowl
the vacant rooms, sniffing the scent of smaller game,
and doing a variegated dance of reclamation. Somehow,
they co-exist harmoniously, these overlords of hunger,
while the ghosts of the three hundred thousand souls
that bastard Amin killed roam the savanna's rough lands
like barren winds. How ephemeral our lives, how
utterly reliant on blind luck and circumstance.

In the Mohave

Nothing sisters me here
but the wide yaw of choice:
shall I be a hermit with blistered feet,
a diviner of dark horizons?
Or a wooly mammoth's ghost?

No, I'd rather haunt a Joshua Tree,
my yucca moth wings aflutter,
and cry out to the moony shadows
sweeping in as I cradle soft pollen
under my chinny-chin-chin.

Thanks be to the parched bogs
of desire that withdraw my breath,
and to this unraveling of hours,
as I roll my giant, compact ball
of pollen into a flower's ovary.

Soon my sturdy larvae will munch
the yucca's fruity seeds while leaf-
nosed bats gobble up my brethren.
My revenge: even time's moth-eaten.
See how the desert listens, deepens.

February Reverie

All day I've watched juncos and chickadees
cling to our hanging feeders to hungrily eat,
while the air's split by hail and wind,

the birds shivering like sailors
swinging on their ships' crossbeams,
their feathers slicked back and darkened.

Nearby, red and grey squirrels war
against each other's tribe, fighting over
acorns they'll later hide in woodpecker holes,

a hundred caches dotting our alders' trunks,
and some filled with acorns so rotten
even ants find them repugnant.

My life's speeding by too fast,
years doubling in me exponentially,
a calculation I can never resolve,

for though each recurring season
offers a pliant rhythm to my days,
something I can't quite name is missing,

though it may be immortality I want.
Or maybe I yearn to craft my thoughts
as mindlessly as the voles who inadvertently

reconfigure our yard's vernal blooms:
daffodils and bluebells springing up
where voles burrowed paths in winter,

moving bulbs underground like volatile
land mines that will explode with color
come April. I'd like that: to be unconscious

of the joys I've planted in others,
and certain that a single kind act won't
stop time, but blossoms outside of it.

Landscape in December

During each full moon the forest shudders,
leaf by leaf, as if some platinum weight
enters the pores of living trees on a cellular level,
dousing them with a heavy, metallic sheen.
Even the marbled boulders wear an afterglow
from that lunar drenching and emanate a cool,
glistening aureole, as from halogen haloes.

How I love to walk outdoors on such nights,
in any season, when the stars step backwards
into silvered shadows, the austere mountains
kindling inner fires as if they're volcanic.

Last winter I took a midnight stroll alone,
meandering along a snow-littered trail aglow
with neon from the waxing moon, and I found
a dying grosbeak, its ochre breast blood-tinged.
Perhaps I'd scared off a coyote, although
the air's quiet veered against this thought.
Reaching for it, I knew I couldn't save it.

Still, I touched its wing lightly before
turning away, leaving it to its frosty rest.
Useless, I thought, to hold what I can't revive.
I see myself now in that bird's glazed eyes—
my puzzled face dark with mortal yearnings.
Overhead, the moon's disguised as a zero,
or else it's eternity's cavernous mouth.

Ode to Fireflies

Dark turns you on,
triggering your sparks,
so that every male who flits
and hovers above summer grass—
each lucent ass dancing out
an insect Morse code—
beckons to a bevy of
hither-coming lasses.

Little flashy, brittle bugs,
you become despair's antidote,
bite-sized asterisks of hope
whose tiny beacons pulsate
through the drifting zones of night,
fueled by pheromones of fire.

I bow to you,
O little souvenirs of awe—
What god or goddess conjured
you from the abyss, set you ablaze
with bioluminescent flashes,
and scented you for sex?
You've taught me how to
wire an electric sizzle
to a good-night kiss.

Transformations

I think of the ibex with her startled eyes,
her onyx horns spiraled into corkscrews,
her shy heart fluttering within barreled ribs.
When she ran, the world became freeze-framed,
as beauty, grace, and power fired the moment
of her very being, as if the ibex was God.

And I recall the tiger's heavy, padded footfalls,
the jungle's hush as she loped, panting and hungry,
across the dirt road, her golden stripes gathering
then widening over taut muscles, her tail articulating
some mystery into throbbing air, a charged secret.
How fields, sky, even umber clouds vanished.

I remember the deer mouse with bulging cheeks
and soft, human hands, how her petal-thin ears
were veined with shivering, delicate threads.
A hawk had dropped her from the sky at my feet.
She licked my palm, eyes glazing with shadows.
Her one word was *no*, squeezed from my throat.

But when I review your birth, daughter, its flood
of waters and blood, your cry staining the darkness,
I see again the animal I labored into this world—
how your luminous skin and black hair secreted
the musk of this earth; I watched your pupils
dilate with the unknown, with my own death.

Now I think of the ibex, tiger, and deer mouse
when I watch you dream in the alpenglow of dusk.
Who will you be in your next life? Or in this one?
You smell like a stranger, both honey and frost.
Though a radiant creature, you want only to step
from your life into a shining beyond yourself.

Gone

Their oceans rose
And their rivers went dry

Bright birds fell
From withered trees

Bees flew backwards
Into the past like arrows

Missing their marks
So pollen turned to ash

While time ran out of
Clocks, or else stood still

Long enough for them
To see everything vanish:

All this world's beauty
Its plangent mystery

Its radiance, sanctity,
Even its memory.

Family Matters

There are only two ways to live your life. One is as if nothing is a miracle. The other is as though everything is a miracle.

—Albert Einstein

Magic Bullets: A Meditation on Loss

Like a slow bullet, an errant clot of blood stopped
a vessel's flow to your brain, Father, and you
became a distant village on an icy winter's night.

It's your familiar thoughts I miss, what fled
before I could say farewell. Your mind, once
my native land, now seems an abandoned plain.

Father, Father, here is my short list of sorrows,
the incense trail my pliant memory draws forth,
while your mind shuffles its scumbled dreams:

- In Fontainebleau, fifty years ago, I followed
  you into a tall forest to cut down a pine for
  the solstice. I asked: *Is the tree's sap its tears?*

- You wept later, our car having struck a doe.
  I'd never seen tears stream down your face,
  nor your shame, and utter speechlessness.

- We all feared your anger, your acerbic tongue.
  It was the adder kept secreted in your voice box,
  its poison sudden, deadly. Where has it gone?

- But music, music! First and last, its beauty
  empowering you for eighty years—you, Father,
  our maestro, tempo tyrant, joy's conductor.

- Those glorious years in Hermosa Beach,
  where the ocean's choirs enlivened us
  as our family strolled along the shore,

❖ you singing along in your perfect alto solo:
"We grow old, we grow old, we shall wear
the bottoms of our trousers rolled…"

❖ Your dark complexity baffling, your moods
an archipelago across whose isles I'd hop,
skip, and jump, so terrified of drowning.

❖ Your winds and currents still a mystery—
your remote terrains, your unspoken griefs.
Were thirty years of adultery an antidote?

❖ How can a brilliant mind take a sabbatical?
Your university lectures made my heart race
around in circles with pride when I was twenty,

❖ for somehow you translated Bach, Brahms, jazz,
and ragas into great monuments of sounds—though
later you said you'd felt stripped naked, deficient.

❖ Haunted your face now, though chiseled, handsome
with your aquiline nose and bright sapphire eyes.
Your mouth's mine, nearly lipless, ever hungry.

❖ Astonishing, a father's strangeness to his daughter.
Twice in a blue moon you'd fired a gun and each
time its blast had jolted you back into the world,

❖ as if the war, the Army, and your fear of dying
awoke in you both the fragility and ferocity of
consciousness. Bullets are emblems both for war

❖ and healing, but I prefer them as glyphs drawn on
the page as leaves, buds, chevrons, or diamonds.
I want your mind back as it was, Father, shining.

Rebuttal

My father wanted me to be masterful as Heifetz,
            playing divertimenti to the crowds;
I hoped to be a country fiddler wooing cows
            back in from pasture—

My father wanted me to be seen, not heard,
            my temper's tempest hurtling towards him;
I yearned to be a forest hermit meditating
            only on being and nothingness;

My father wished I'd been a son: brave, strong,
            a testament to his testosterone, but, alas,
I was born his daughter and named myself
            simply another Simon.

If he could see me from beyond his urn,
            would Dad unfurl my name with pride?
Would he recognize himself in my aging face,
            forgive his own father his wounding words?

I see my girlhood mien, ablaze with indignant rage,
            and also, my present self, scathed by regret,
worn smooth by grinding years—a fingerprint,
            its whorls fading from my ablutions.

Now I long for my father's voice to ring out
            in any timbre—for him to scold me again
for every misdemeanor, even for being
            a felonious girl—just to hear his noise.

No Wars Are Won

Because someone always dies who's
innocent, and someone else accidentally kills
his brother, and another soldier surrenders to
a darkness so profound it blinds his regiment.

Wars leave so much wreckage that even
vultures feel overwhelmed, scavenger dogs
get glutted with remorse, and silent battle scars
reappear in succeeding generations when
our grandchildren's nightmares revisit
their elders' war trauma.

No wars are won when scorched battlefields
lie fallow for decades, poisoned by toxins,
when enemies pretend they're reconciled,
when they're simply muted by grief.

My father's war made him feel lucky
to be alive, though he never left the "islands,"
Staten and Manhattan, and despised the Army.
Your father's battles won him a Bronze Star,
a Purple Heart, shrapnel in his back, and worse,
PTSD that he's passed on to you, his son—

Because your dad's kin were murdered by Nazis,
his was a "good war," he said. I disagree, for
how can any war be worthy when both sides
lose their moral compass—when slain bodies
blanket earth, blindly sowing despair's seeds?

A Philosophical Argument

Some miracles are mistakes,
or merely uncanny coincidences.
Take, for example, what happened
after Jesus turned stones into loaves
of challah and brought forth a shoal
of fish at the Sea of Tiberias: some
of his disciples got food poisoning;
others completely lost their appetites
for forty days and nights. Manna
that's materialized from thin air
apparently has a short shelf life.

Or take the holy one's famous stroll
across the glassy Sea of Galilee:
there'd been a strange freeze that
night, turning the water's meniscus
into ice. Yes, Jesus walked upon
that frozen water's crinkled shelf:
afterward, his callused feet turned
blue briefly with frostbite.

And it was an algae bloom that
turned the Nile's waters blood-red,
not Moses with his sturdy staff
wielding his god-imbued magic.

And the shroud of Turin resulted
not from a miraculous imprint
of Jesus, postmortem, but from
the hand of a Gothic artist who'd
bought a length of herringbone twill
from an Indian tradesman, and then
fashioned a long-limbed impression
of Jesus on it. Also, anatomically, it's
impossible for a corpse lying prostrate

to cover his genitals with his hands.

But there are bona fide miracles,
I admit, like April's explosion of
apricot blossoms on our ancient tree,
and the way Adélie penguins can
migrate over 8,000 miles each year
to the Ross Sea in Antarctica. Even

your loving me seems like a miracle,
since fifty years of dealing with my
idiosyncrasies and foibles would tax
the strongest heart, and yet your love
brings forth metaphorical starfish and
baguettes galore; it turns my cheeks
red with desire, the blood in all my
tiny capillaries dilating like angelic
choirs singing on high; and your
good face imprints its tenderness
daily on the linen of my hours.

Unfinished Poem

If there's some truth to be found
in suffering, I don't know what it is,
unless it's that the darkest stars burn

brightest as they implode, so rather
than being diminished by our pain,
we're enlarged by a clarity grief brings.

Consider those pods of beached whales
who die helplessly in the shore's surf,
refusing to abandon an ailing fellow—

their needless deaths seem more tragic
because they're honoring succor over
self-survival, because their loyalty

and love will turn them into the kind
of martyrs none of us want to be.
What's the truth of such suffering,

if not that these intelligent beings
understand sacrifice in the same way
that Ukrainian soldiers do, and that

my mother did, when she whispered,
Even if your sorrow's unbearable,
I won't stay alive for you any longer—

Pain Log #1

Everywhere the nerves pulse with it,
And the self shrivels, and the spirit
Dwindles. Still, the fingers peck out
This tired lament, and outside
In the dark, the rainbow trout swim
In languorous circles.

Pain Log #2: Letter to My Sister

I listen to Arvo Pärt's sacred music
and think of his native Estonia,
which reminds me of that Estonian
lawyer and historian whom I met
one November at the American
Academy in Rome. She wore
an outlandish costume for our
communal dinners—mauve taffeta
suit with matching hat—and she
had a flat face and cold affect.
Ingeniously, she found ways to
direct any conversation back to
jaw-dropping stereotypes: Jews
were stealing all of Europe's wealth,
the unclean Jews from her home-
town, "stink like horse shit," and
"Jews are taking all the good jobs."
Our table of diners grew silent,
shocked and embarrassed by
her casually professed hatred.

So, I conclude that Estonia, like any
country, is capable of producing
both enlightened men like Arvo Pärt
and highly intelligent hate-mongers.
The body, too, produces joy machines
like endorphins (absent right now),
and cells bent on destroying their
neighbors. We always inhabit or
contain at least two worlds
simultaneously.

Pain Log #5

If you suffer long enough—
until your thoughts blister,
your body fractures at touch,
and your face caves in—
eventually you'll turn into
either a monster of despair
or a saint of compassion.

This is what I've learned so
far along this jagged journey
that has yet to broadcast a
single happy ending in my ear.
They do exist, I'm told. Still,
you never know if you'll
succumb to being a sufferer

whose darkness is a contagion
to the world, or if you'll be trans-
formed into a bringer of light,
a graced soul who ignites all
the faces your being touches.
Perhaps it's possible to be both:
a strange pushmi-pullyu hybrid

who wears a crooked halo above
a face beaten into a pulp by pain.
I think not, for the separate roads
taken by the stricken seem never
to converge. I say, always be kind
to whomever hurts, friend and
enemy alike. To yourself first.

Pain Log #7

Who can know what awaits us
at day's end, or at week's end,
or at the end of our singular lives?
Will beauty still widen our pupils,
and awaken our nerves with fire?

Will our shadows gracefully balance
themselves on invisible tightropes
beneath our heels, playing at being
human, though made of a substance
that denies its own flesh and bone?

Not starlight, but maybe the soul's
own illumination ignites a new path
for us to follow when darkness
overwhelms us, when the echoes
of fallen selves beckon us to follow.

Spindrift

My love, these days are a current towing
us through a sea of longing, every gaze
untethering whitely from the blue blaze
of mirrors, our desire gathering a going
forward, then an uprising, then a falling
down onto emptied shores: can we unlace
us from the lunar pull of each other's face,
and daily keep our selves from shattering?
Let's become islands instead of breakers,
part of a curved archipelago's arm
flung by a molten, geologic bellows—
so that our days of yearning cross wide acres,
instead of leagues, so that there's no harm
in drowning together briefly in the shallows.

Space Dot : A Love Letter

O · darling · long before · our partition · I saw you · as

A bright wafer · a pixel of hope · a jot of gold · an iota of air

My gumdrop · interpunct · a mustard seed · implanted · in crystal

Icon of transit · love's cinder · sweet crumb · a pinpoint of light

My savory dewdrop · I saw · a flickering · in your green eyes

I saw · your *leof* face · a flowering disk · afloat · in blue ether

Your sly mouth · supple and moist · so sensual · a neural feast

I touched · your cheeks · their stubble · their salty heat · and

All · seemed suspended · my hewn life · my heartbeat · even

My breath · so that · death · collapsed · momentarily and

Always · it withdrew · into an acorn · into a tiny stye · dotting

The moon's eyelid · and only · your tender touch · your flesh

To awaken · my life · O · darling · long before · our partition

A Lament for My Elders

I would have hefted heaven and earth aloft
        to keep your hearts thumping in your thorny chests,
your world-weary lungs filling like accordions,
        your eyes shining with visions pierced by glee.

But you performed your leave-taking dutifully—
        such are nature's commandments, its ordained cycles—
so, though your vanishing slowed my life with sorrow,
        I no longer saw you in the wavering shadows

of each waking day, but gazed forward wearily,
        instead, to my own journey into these waning years.
When I held my friend's newborn grandson yesterday,
        watching his fitful sleep, his delicate eyelids trembling

like moths over the incandescent light of his dreams,
        I saw my dying mother's face as she wandered inside
and outside of herself, a mind-traveller breeching
        the space-time continuum, free to leap-frog between

childhood and marriage, her prime and senescence,
        as if she'd already sloughed off her body to be free.
She huddles in my heart, a lost immigrant, as dazed
        as I am, yet somehow fortified by eternity.

Where can I store you all—my irredeemable losses?
        I turn to you now, when the world seems cursed
with its own demise, when suffering's endemic:
        lift me up high upon your invisible shoulders.

What I Was Taught

1.
My girlish body: a keg of
gunpowder awaiting a boy's
glance to ignite, his thoughts
fueling it with an incendiary
wallop, and all I need do is
cover my skin with shame,
seal my taut lips, swallow my
pride, bite my tongue, then
smile as Any Boy sniffs my
shadow, trails me like a dog,
hungry, panting, and aching
for that explosion I've surely
laid as a booby trap for him.

2.
When they speak first in class,
as they always do, cutting off
my quiet words and loud ideas,
I pretend not to care, pretend I'm
so impressed by their braininess,
by their brilliant boyish blather.

3.
Being thin is a virtue that's
equal in value to a girl's face,
which needs to be pleasing.
Large breasts are important,
too, as is an abundant ass.
Be dime-thin, yet buxom as
a pin-up girl, yet be demure.

4.
I said to myself: what does it
matter what the body is for—
getting me from sink to desk,
pushing food down its throat
then shitting out the calories,
bleeding every month like a
Fertility Machine. Why study
Latin? French? Math? Poetry?

5.
Who starts the wars, I thought.
Who bloodies each other on
every schoolyard, who catcalls
after me like I'm errant cattle?

6.
Hey, girl, do you hear me?
I'm talking to you, so stop
walking away. You can't be
here, you can't walk here.
Look at me, you whore, you
fucking idiot piece of shit.

7.
I studied the Salem witch trials.
Thirty convicted, fourteen girls
and women condemned as
Satan's instruments: executed
by hanging for staring too long
at the full moon, or surviving a
fall down the stairs, for spinning

too fine a linen, or, like Bridget
Bishop, a frequenter of taverns,
for dressing flamboyantly and
being thrice married.

8.
I watched as boys and teachers
put down and shut out (or shut up)
those headstrong girls with their
sassy tongues, the brilliant mimes,
boldest tomboys—I learned about
men's terror of female power,
about our violent past,
our brutal heritage,
our legacies of hate
still so alive.

9.
You Cow, you Dog, you Bitch,
You Harpy, Pussy, Cunt, you
Bossy Ball-buster, you shrill,
Castrating Shrew, Man-hating
Ice Queen, Feminazi, Cock-tease,
Frigid Slut, you hysterical Old
Crow, you hormonal, neurotic,
Sleazy Skank, you Douchebag,
Strident and catty Jail Bait—
You're asking for it...

10.
My girlish body
a thing
to be toyed with
grabbed by jocks
in high school corridors

a thing not wholly mine
shameful secret
boy-magnet with
its poisoned heart
maimed dreams—
so unlike Circe's body
or Athena's armored flesh
or fierce Kali with her
blood-curdling fangs—

11.
A woman in the shape of a monster
a monster in the shape of a woman
the skies are full of them.

A Palindromic Life

The opposite of a fact is falsehood,
but the opposite of one profound truth
may very well be another profound truth.

—Niels Bohr (Danish physicist)

Saturday Night Fever

Sine amore, nihil est vita.

"You're a better zombie than I am,"
the straggler says to me
as we thousands surge into
a blockaded village,
our wounds weeping, our chorus
of groans rising steadily
into a thunderous crescendo.

"That's because I'm hungrier,"
I confess to her, "so ravenous
I'd eat a morgue full of
skinny lap dancers." Grinning,
we swarm the electric fencing,
engulf the townsfolk who yelp
like baby rabbits.

The fallen lie still for moments only
before they struggle into
their newly made, clumsy personas,
looking like us now: hollow-eyed,
weak, absurd, unstoppable.
"Every Saturday night
the apocalypse arrives anew
atop our shoulders," I mutter
to the slowpoke whose mouth looks
like the black hole of Calcutta.

"Can zombies fall in love?"
she asks sweetly, then spits out
clumps of someone's scalp.
"Death has few rules," I admit,
"besides making us tragic
anti-heroes who are mostly inept,
and immoral, or, rather,

I mean—*immortal*." She giggles,
"a double whammy!" We clasp hands
as we lunge forward together,
panting, hungry for life.

Quotation Marks: A Bestiary

A sprinkling of New Year's confetti

First trickle of nuptial rice

Dandruff flung from Tom Thumb's pate

White lies afloat *in media res*

Clothespins clipped to a fishing line

Silence tacked to the page

Footprints left by a tiny two-toed sloth

Two pinches of baby nail clippings

Dimples on the household wraith

The Invisible Man's dialogue with himself

A skirl of errant raindrops

Double-digit deflation

Duos of inchworms do-si-do-ing

Enigmatic scars on a surfer's chin

Iron filings marching toward war's magnet

Basting stitches hemming a thought

Four eyelashes wept into a handkerchief

A Theory of Eyebrows

I.

With pipe bombs wedged in their baby's backpack,
the wedded San Bernardino terrorists sped away
from their targets, their black pupils dilating from
an aftermath of vengeful murder—their eyebrows
drooping parentheses to those hate-enveloped eyes,
their retinas shattering into icy splinters as they
were shot, their eyebrows beading with blood.

II.

Adolph Hitler's eyebrows wouldn't accept
the brow-beatings by his father: out he plucked them,
hair by hair, each night and planted them underneath

his dresser's daily folded, ironed underwear.
But Adolph's eyebrows grew back more massive
and bristly than a boar's, became ever more

abhorrent to him, became iron weights—
those eyebrows redolent of imminent death,
the source of his profound shame.

III.

A little-known fact: a redhead, a brunette, a blonde,
and (predictably) a black-haired rider, the four weary
Horsemen of the Apocalypse used their scythes
to shave off their bristling eyebrows, then waxed
and sharpened them to use as secret weapons—
ingenious and multi-colored—razors, needles,
tiny ice picks, miniature daggers.

IV.

And don't forget the pale eyebrows of Petra Laszlo,
that Hungarian broadcaster who tripped a Syrian man
and his small boy, bedraggled refugees, as they fled
to freedom: two weeks later, her cute eyebrows
turned into skin lice and chewed off half her face.

V.

Of course, Kim Jong Un's black "baronet" hairstyle
—hair shaved off the sides and back of his head,
hair jelly-rolled into a mini-tsunami up on top—
caused his eyebrows to contract to half
their normal size. Thus, his doctors surgically
removed his traumatized, truncated eyebrows,
replacing them with a self-regenerating fungus
that, sadly, stinks like raw sewage.

VI.

Joe Stalin's hirsute brows were powered
by a genetic link to a Neanderthal tribe
which practiced ritualized infanticide
of male newborns with jade green eyes
or ungainly noses: that was most offspring
born each fall—a terrible slaughter.

Hence, Stalin's penchant for brutality,
mayhem, the starvation of millions,
and his remarkably stalwart eyebrows.

It's an open secret that, after his death
and embalming, Stalin's eyebrows detached
themselves, as he lay in state, then slid off

his corpulent face and, like inchworms, moved
down his trousers to his shrunken genitals,
where they set up shop selling tiny squares
of rotting flesh on the black market
to bereft yet grateful mourners. Today,
those minute computer chips of cruelty,
when dropped in a glass of water, detonate
as powerfully as a not-so-smart bomb.

VII.

Once a stately black unibrow, my own eyebrows
separated in middle age, and now appear as mere
shadows of their former selves. No longer am I
mistaken for a pale Frieda Kahlo; no more taunts
by my wisecracking daughters. My eyebrows turn
grayer and grayer, like mold on yogurt.
Still, there's always a lesson to be had:
countering our moral turpitude, eyebrows
serve as our faces' stewards, twin sentries
of truth, fine chaperones of our integrity.
Don't try to fool them: their power is divine.

The Slash

Razor-smart and long as a sailor's arm
waved one last time above water before
drowning, the slash catapults itself aslant
the line/page/mind—a 10-degree tilt

that only a flagless country would raise,
wishing against despair that someone somewhere
would re-erect its purpose, and join forces/
intent/import to a cause as common as hope.

True, the slash has slyly reinvented itself into
hypertext, becoming a signifier to circuitry,
a swinging door/way/latch that divides and
multiplies letters/integers/words like knives.

Don Quixote's lance/ship's sinking mast/
Hitler's heil/snow-bent daffodil/tombstone
leaning into death/shaftless arrow/swordsman's
cheek-borne scar/lightning's gash renting the dark.

A Palindromic Life

Hannah ate a banana and said to her sis,
Ada, I want to be a racecar driver, or else
a kayak rider who floats under the radar.

Ada replied, *Wow, don't nod yes to being*
an avid diva or a drab bard when you might
stab bats midflight as a witch, or edit the tide—

be magical like a decal-laced dog god. Jeez,
Hannah muttered, *you've got delusions of*
grandeur. I tubed my début as a kook who

spoke Malayalam, so now I'll swallow pride
and level my gaze toward a civic vocation,
though I stink in knits. But at night I'll retool

as a looter and live an evil life! Ada shook off
her mood of doom, nibbled the nub of a bun,
and said, *Oh ho, you can slap pals for a living,*

that is, recite sagas at noon to your co-workers,
and grow redder with shame than a fireplug.
Shite, I'd murder for a jar of red rum right now.

Ada stood, said, *Our deified mom's arrived*
wearing the bib of a nun. Talk about weird.
Hannah whispered, *Ma is as selfless as I am.*

LOL, said Ada, *I think I'm going to gag.*
Put on that DVD of solos by Rats Star, ok?
But Hannah was dreaming again of sloops

and spools, of ruby Sedna and the far Andes.
Borrow or rob, I'll be the Suez Zeus, or else
an oozy rat in a sanitary zoo. A tattarrattat

at the front door interrupted the girls' noon:
a man was saying to their mom, "Madam,
it's too hot to hoot, but don't nod *No* yet."

A salesman again! Hannah ran to Mom's aid,
shouted, *No sir, away! A papaya war is on!*
Then she added, *Yo, banana boy!* Sometimes

acting crazy's the best life tenet, Hannah mused.
Dammit, I'm mad, her mom said sotto voce,
looking upset. *Did you eat UFO tofu again?*

she demanded. *You're like Camus on Sumac!*
Mom had such smug gums; she'd repel a leper.
A gut tug. *So many dynamos in this family.*

No Passports to Heaven

No socks for the freezing feet of saints
No hallelujahs for bereaved housewives
No dimples for newly glazed windows
No safety nets for trapezing spiders
No epiphanies for the lotus eaters
No way out of waywardness
No time but the pheasant's
No book but your secret longings
No darkness without illumination
No maps to the starving starlets
No exit through hellfire's mazes
No murderous plots for resurrection
No Necco wafers from the Pope
No rest for the pickets
No rest for the bleary
No place like Rome
No shirt, no surfeit
No iron shackles for transgressors
Noh theater masks, but no kabuki
No trespassing into Eden
No free tickets to the madhouse
No twitters to God

Post-Pleistocene Blues

Cheetahs once wandered the jungles of Nebraska,
alongside other megafauna like short-faced bears
and lumbering Columbian mammoths.

Herds of these pachyderms waded into a vast lake
in southeast Dakota's savannas, and drowned
after being sucked into quicksand mud.

Over millennia, they fused into a many-storied
high-rise of fossilized skulls, rib cages, and tusks.
Though time's a finite resource, some species
squander it, like us.

Sheelah-Na-Gig

Carved as the keystone in this wayside church,
she presides over passersby who, when gazing
upward toward God or the stars, see, instead,
a nude woman with bent knees spread apart,
her hands opening her vulva like a doorway.

Her ribs are lean, deeply incised; her breasts
dangle like whey-filled sacks dripping two
large droplets about to splash down with
loud splats. Her bald, triangular head tilts
its skull defiantly toward sinner and faithful

alike, as if the owlish, intense eyes know some-
thing dark about the soul that we'd sooner
forget. But it's her gaping mouth that stops
my breath—for Sheelah howls the rage of
a girl betrayed, or with a sexual joy defying

time and place, oblivious to eons of voyeurs.
Or maybe her wail's the virgin's shriek having
been violently speared, or she yowls in agony,
squatting in childbirth, the amniotic sac having
just burst. Her expression, though so public,

mirrors in its depth the private parts of
her exposed and perpetual metamorphosis:
goddess, hag, whore, queen of the pagans,
angelic demon, naked warrior of the Lord,
and turnstile to the before-and-after world.

@: A Triptych

(with thanks to Giorgio Stabile)

On May 4, 1536, the Venetian merchant,
Francesco Lapi, documented the sale of his wine

to one Signore Pizarra @ so many gold Florins
per litre, just as centuries earlier in Rome

a monk named Ambrosius bent over his accounts
for the monastery larder: twenty bags of flour

@ such-and-such a price, plus ten amphorae of oil
@ a preposterous amount, given their market value—

but he and his brothers were beholden to their vendor,
first cousin of the Abbot, and thus Ambrosius

bent over his parchment tally and carefully
devised this glyph in his Latin hand.

*

It's so mercantile a sign, this @, and yet it morphs
iconically through time, appearing as: a squashed raisin

or a minute egg nestled in a cup, as a meager cabbage or
a sleeping cat, as a Cinnabun, mini-cyclone, petite rose,

or a *Schnabel* (a German *beak*, my friend Siegfried tells me),
or as a scroll, a strudel, (*das ist gut*, says you-know-who),

or as a monkey tail, eyeball, vortex, whorl, a whirlpool—
I see @ as a paper nautilus beached after a storm,

its tenant weary, marooned, who looks up
to a night sky vaster than death and swirling

wildly with asterisks to see mirrored
in our galaxy her home's perfect spiral.

*

Nowadays, the @ sign adorns everyone but God's
email address, ever blinking its Cyclops eye at us—

Its lens never closes, rarely blinks, rigidly staring
out with its gaze of a mini god, a tiny tyrant.

I believe @ was the Ur-computer's birthmark,
begot from the vast cosmos of cyberspace.

Now it's apparent everywhere, a genetic marker
that's proliferated like dust mites and twitches—

But once, centuries ago, @ spilt like a droplet
of red wine from a Roman merchant's flask,

as a monk named Ambrosius toasted a sale,
the firmament, the rich vineyards ripening

beyond his stone walls, and divine providence.

Ten Things I Know Are True

1. That zero holds in its pouch an infinite number of pregnant thoughts

2. That death has three handmaidens: disbelief, sorrow, and assent—
   but only the latter believes in rebirth

3. That autumn's ruby-haired herald bears a fragrance of decomposing dreams:
   she signals the hibernations of fence lizards and demi-gods

4. That gravity keeps our bodies from levitating towards the Milky Way,
   which, like the sky, spills itself from itself

5. That taxes are a joke for the rich and a millstone or gallows for the poor

6. That war will forever rear its ugly, malformed head and bellow
   like Cronus for more children to eat

7. That chocolate was Mexico's gift to its Spanish conquerors,
   while smallpox was Hernando Cortez's legacy to the Aztecs

8. That hearing children's spangly voices and chiming laughter
   lowers our blood pressure and increases our endorphins

9. That despair wears Medusa's hair

10. That each skyscape is mystical: today's neon blue could be a trick
    up God's sleeve, or else an open door to unbeing

Untold Lives of Ancient Greece

Lasthenia of Mantinea
    was Plato's brightest lady student.
A cross-dresser, she rode upon
    a dappled horse to each morning's
Academy symposium and
    wore her linen tunic short,

fastening it with a bull-head brooch,
    as was men's fashion in Athens,
so she could dismount freely.
    Her woolen cloak was purple, her broad-
brimmed hat yellow, her earrings
    beaten from Egyptian gold.

A papyrus fragment from Oxyrhynchus
    states: "in her teens, Lasthenia was
lovely and full of unstudied grace."
    It fails to describe her acerbic wit,
her analyses of ethical treatises,
    her lyric rhyming couplets.

After Plato died, Lasthenia studied
    with Plato's nephew, Speussipus,
with whom she'd linger after class,
    exchanging kisses in a scroll closet
after the other students left.
    They enjoyed a long romance,

often exchanging clothes,
    since Speussipus fancied ladies'
silk chitons that draped down to
    his ankles and other artifices,
like the sleeved robes that actors
    wore or adder-skin belts.

Lasthenia of Mantinea co-
    wrote her teacher's famed treatise,
On Pythagorean Numbers,
    but never received credit for it,
nor for their "mathematics of reality"
    she organized into spiritual spheres.

Lasthenia bore three dutiful daughters
    who disdained learning,
as well as horseback riding, who stayed home
    and dressed as proper ladies.
Her only son, Timaeus, enjoyed pederasty
    with his young slaves,

one of whom grandfathered
    Aesop, Greek fabulist and slave
of African descent, advisor to
    kings, writer of six hundred fables
with apt morals. For stealing a gold cup,
    Aesop was thrown off a cliff.

Gyn-Ecology

1.
Strange Things

Two enormous breasts hang over the world
like dangling atom bombs, though these
leviathans promise Niagara Falls of milk,
not obliteration, nor radiation everlasting.

What's their topography, you ask?
Their skin's tautly stretched, as if they're
tribal drum skins, supple as summer and
nicely tanned. Their shape's pendulous,

and the larger left breast bears a mole
the size of Cincinnati on its underside.
Their nipples boast pale strawberry-fawn
aureoles that match a conch's inner hue.

These gigantic mamillae swivel over our
deserts like roving UFOs, causing some
alarm before they unleash milky deluges
over barren lands and into empty dams.

To whom do they belong, these floating
grands tétons and drought-proof melons?
To an ancient Colossus circumnavigating
earth in search of love? Or to a reincarnation

of Gaia, come to nurse humankind back
to robust health? No, they exist simply
as themselves, disembodied from a Self,
and they seem intent on flooding us

either with a hungering shame, with lust,
or gob-smacking awe. At night they float

across the sky like gibbous moons. They've
been heard to moan like marooned sailors.

2.
Regina Vagina

A yoni wears the nicest pout and,
if denuded of hair, reminds me
of the vertical, fashionable grin
of a closed silk opera purse.

Mysterious envelope exuding
a musky perfume, its fleshy tunnel
softens and moistens at the hint
of desire, swelling voluptuously

to meet with bravada its lover's
tumescence. Queen consort to
the velvet metra, her diadem's a
tiny tidal wave triggering ecstasy.

What a surprise when my aging tuft
turned white as a lab mouse ready
to scurry off to an afterlife that's
reserved solely for changelings.

3.
Uterine Schemes

What is a womb if not a buoyant boat
afloat inside our bodies as it awaits
a tiny passenger who'll sail into
the arms of this world?

That little Argonaut encapsulated
in my womb sucked her thumb,
dreamt of an earlier life,
and hummed to herself

a tune so Ur-otherworldly that,
had I overheard it in this blue
oxygenated air, I'd know
I'd spawned an alien.

But I forget myself: the womb's
what I'm concerned with here—
in essence, it serves as a soft
conveyance for humanity,

acting not unlike a Jill-in-the-box
with its little stowaway, a vessel
winding itself up for 9 months
until—voilà!—*out-pops-a-miracle.*

My uterus seems lonely these days;
I suspect she yearns to be reunited
with her absentminded ovaries,
her stoppered fallopian tubes.

She still dreams of the babes whom
she carried: miniature seafarers
riding out unique destinies,
and whom she launched

with regret into our atmosphere,
knowing that every traveler
would ultimately be fleeced
by some golden pursuit.

4.
But Consider the Clitoris,

what every infant girl's blessed
to possess as part of her own sacred
anatomy, the jewel in her vulva's tiara,

so to speak, and a pinpoint for peak
pleasure, a little nub-kins to rub
when lonely or horny or just bored.

With 12,000 nerve endings, thrice as
many as its chum, the penis, the clit
bestows to us a rubied pleasure dome—

what an ancient Greek locksmith
dubbed the "key" to a lady's arousal—
with its hood and legs and bulbs,

with its wishbone-shaped form that
becomes an engorged orchid when
tickled and nudged and stroked.

Doorbell for delirium, blushingly
rosy anther, pert pearl of longing,
we share you with ostriches,

turtles, lemurs, moles, hyenas,
and bonobos. O blessèd nether
knurl, you hold a divine power

to catapult us into ecstasy's pyre,
a place we'll inhabit so briefly—
yet each second's an eternity.

Rules of Thumb

1
There's no such thing as an idle rumor:
it festoons itself with ribbons, spurs,
then buckles its belt and gets to work.
Or it travels the air, an invisible rope,
tying knots in people's throats.
It lassos the proud in mid-run,
knocking them down to the ground.
It can lay low the mighty in a day,
raise the obscure to brief infamy.
The only feat it can't complete is,
as yet, unheard of.

2
Nobody loves moralists,
least of all their mothers,
who noticed how often,
after birth, their babes turned
from their proffered nipples
which were taut as buttons
on elevator doors.
Nobody loves moralists
despite the fact that they
shook their fingers at their fathers
when their fathers went off to wars.
Nobody loves moralists, least of all
the moralists themselves, who,
for all their stern objections,
know that moralists are bores.

3
Stones cannot be tamed,
but men can be broken like mules,
and emptied of their souls.
How can we stop ourselves
from growing into headless nails?
We must be blind again, be deaf,
be dumb, be reborn ad infinitum.

4
God, put a pox on every money box
that isn't mine. At the end
of the month the bills rush in
like a flock of paper pigeons
with sharp talons and stools
that burn holes in all my linens.
The bills are building a monument
of shit, and daily I must climb it.
God, put a pox on every money box
that isn't mine, or else
uninvent the clock.

5
The rules of thumb are double-jointed,
but the rules of fingers are single-minded.
The index finger points away from the I,
as the middle finger flips off the Other.
Ring finger, caught as it is around its waist,
doesn't bother with distinctions, being
wed to the finger of its doppelgänger.
Only the pinkie knows what it's for:
tiny oar pinpointing the stars.

The Blue Bridge

To what shall I
compare the world?
It's like the wake
vanishing behind a boat
that has rowed away at dawn.

—Sami Manzei (8th c. Buddhist monk)

The Blue Bridge

The most dangerous time is the most spiritual.
-Chumash elder

Heaving winds scatter stars across the sky,
while below its light-pitted dome,
tall cedars shiver, rattling parched branches.
I stand in winter's darkness, alone
beneath two chittering, invisible wrens—
and I hold a secret in my throat.

Once a woman sailed upstairs to paint
these constellations—my mother with
her black braid flying behind her, a kite's tail.
I feel her floating down to earth slowly,
landing softly beside me, where she sighs,
Oh, if only I could stay a while.

It's fire season all year long now,
and as these Santa Ana winds howl,
the forest's trees daven like a thousand rabbis
beseeching an erstwhile god. I want to shout
these gales into oblivion, or wrestle them
into an abyss, then quickly shut its lid.

In an eyelid's blink, a match put to these woods
could cause a conflagration so vast
it would smoke out the Milky Way, char our lives
beyond recognition. We jeopardize nature,
and it's fighting back. I used to think life
always wins, but my mind's changed now:

we've lost too much wilderness. Too many ghosts
harangue us for abandoning them, for severing
ourselves from nature: they return to warn us.
And I see a catwalk stretching out before us,
a road to redemption. Its hue is otherworldly,
tinged a rare morning-glory-blue.

This sky-yearning bridge, this umbilicus,
    joins our sorrow to a splintered radiance.
My brave mother knows its truth, and though
    dead, she travels silently back and forth
riding her zip-line and tethered to hope—
    a taste of the afterlife wetting her tongue.

Midsummer's Day

(Visby, Sweden)

Being secretive, the Baltic Sea suggests
a formal surrender, its slate back turned
obliquely from the sky. Its waters seem,
at once, placid and in perpetual disquiet,
as if some great truth stirred below them,
a wisdom so profound, its surface
shudders with echoes.

All day the bells of St. Mary's sound
in counterpoint to the swallows' chittering,
to the blackbirds' mellifluous songs.

It's the longest day in the middle of my life,
and I awaken to it as if to another dream,
one in which the sails of skiffs are voices
propelled by God. So brief our days among
the holy beauties, where great limestone arches
bend like maidens to the pull of the earth
beneath the Milky Way's invisible arms.

May we be like those great windmills
perched on the cliffs, continually turning
over our groans and grievances to the wind,
and dwelling in the baroque silence
of our own souls.

On Some Hand-Me-Downs from G-d

Well, mortality's one of the cloaks you tossed in the bin,
as well as sin, I suppose, and all this endless yearning
for some divine inspiration. You also tossed forgiveness
into the Goodwill box, so casually I'd have thought it was
a pair of dirty socks. But there's another inheritance I
guess I ought to thank you for—faith—though it's worn
so thin and ragged it's nearly diaphanous, like a nylon
banner hung out for eons from the roof of the world.
You kept all the best stuff for yourself: universal health
insurance, archangels, Capuchin monks and Capuchine
nuns, eternal life, 4-D sunglasses, that pristine garden
with its sagacious fruit and peaceable kingdom. In short,
you live in splendor, at least metaphorically, and we
mortals go from thrift store to consignment shop
hoping we'll find some treasure you forgot to hoard.

Residency

Does a person's soul rise like a throng of fireflies
from the cold body's vessel, forming as it soars
a cloud of forgetfulness that floats unseen
above sorrowing mourners?

Does that whirlwind, freed by gravity,
glow with the light of living breath, as if
fueled by a great oak's green-hearted thrust,
its movement a surge of premonition?

Surely each vibrating cloud—golden
as a cache of glittering wings—reforms
miraculously into a microscopic soul.
Later it slips into a womb-entombed embryo

smaller than a sesame seed. And then?
A long sigh of being will issue from new lips
as the child's blood-swelled chamber resounds
with two beating hearts. Even in its amnesia,

its tiny mind swims with possibility,
and hope clings to its skin like vernix.

One Voice

I felt a god's wing brush my shoulder this evening
as I strolled along Via Appia Antica. A Sunday dusk,
Rome's cobbled road was devoid of cars, and a twilit
hush filled my ears when I passed Priscilla's Tomb.

A peacefulness sifted through me, as if the dust of
two thousand years infused my living cells with light.

Was it Apollo, god of poetry, who grazed my skin
with his invisible wing, hovering near me and
pausing mid-flight like a suspended thought?

Tall umbrella trees cast islands of darkness
all around me, and I felt a sigh singe the air
as his gaze rested on the curve of my neck.

A breeze stirred my hair. A grey swan rose out
of a meadow near the road, a triumphant omen.

It's true my pen can't recover the veiled thoughts
of the catacombs' eternal guests, but it can raise gods
from their iron sepulchers, defying the physics
of gravity and time. It can make love fly again.

Creation Redux

Every moment of light and dark is a miracle. -Walt Whitman

When God composed what we call day,
he used a pen engorged with blue delight
and ink-stained with bright incandescence.
He tore a page from the Milky Way's spiraling
tail for his scroll, flattening that cosmic wave till
a prophetic tongue unfurled to jump-start time.
He pulled night from a black hole's depths,
fraught with compressed gravity and stellar winds.

God was young then, having dreamed himself
into being like a gigantic sunflower bulging with seeds.
He hoped to do things right: to auger a world so lustrous
it would blind even the stars. Most he loved the sparks
of beauty he launched within both ocean and sky
and across undulating lands: variegated creatures
crawling, swimming, hopping, flying, galloping,
or running for their lives.

"Come to me, children," God whispered each dawn,
"and you'll grow ripe and wise." But they ran from him
at first, escaping his shadow that hovered over them,
an ominous black cumulus. Fearing his powerful gaze,
they knew they'd no choice but to bide their time
and hide their fright in obedient acts.
Yet, after eons, his creatures moved toward
acceptance of their fates, their mortality.

I know you won't believe me when I tell you
how quickly God aged, how his years piled up
like a tower of autumn leaves. His white beard flowed
down from Annapurna in waves of avalanching snow,
flooding the Indo-Gangetic Plain. His teeth yellowed.
He yearned for his youthful sleight of hand,
as when his snapped fingers spawned tardigrades,
those minuscule water bears defying starvation.

But now his mind felt cobwebbed, ancient.
His hips and knees always ached; his energy flagged.
God grew weary of being omnipotent and, worse,
he felt remorseful about abandoning his people.
It had all been a mistake, so he decided to make
creation null and void, to undo it step-by-step.
It took him a week, and he wept while he worked.
Such a vast erasure! Then he undid himself.

The Widow

Come back. Even as a shadow,
even as a dream. -Euripides

How slippery is the pained road to Wednesday,
when Tuesday hasn't yet grinded to a halt,
and Monday only took its last breath seconds ago—
snapping it out like a piece of stale gum.
Sunday seems as distant as an icicle shimmering
in hell, and Saturday must have taken the elevator
to the basement of grief, where the cobwebs grow.
I know Friday was so carnivorous it swallowed
itself whole, and Thursday—yes, Thursday—
magenta, torn, halted, crazed, untranscendent,
too much, never enough, forever-ever bleating
like a slaughtered sheep—oh, Thursday
was the day you vanished, my belovèd,
then time fell apart.

States of Being

The very concepts of exact position and exact velocity together have no meaning in nature. -Werner Heisenberg

My father's an ambidextrous Don Juan
singing with perfect pitch while
watering his bougainvillea.

My mother's an artist who paints
pensive pelicans and warbles off-tune.
Her dungarees are livid with acrylics.

My sister's lavender eyes ache
from all the sadness in her life—
she dreams of eating escargots in Paris.

My husband's body hurts constantly
from arthritis, but his brain writhes
from American politics.

My elder daughter's losing her mind
in the courthouse, though she still loves
how the law bends towards justice.

My younger kid nurses cancer-razed
patients at work; at home, she teaches
her three dogs how to sit perfectly still.

Me, I'm matter-of-factly facing
my mortality with a grain of soot
and a teaspoon of raw *ayahuasca.*

Always hovering nearby, the Devil
watches each of us with casual interest
as he winds and unwinds his watch.

Further away, sitting atop a baobab tree,
the Angel of Empathy scribbles notes
on her eternally smooth kneecap.

She writes: "Alas, they are all falling
behind in achieving a divine order,
but we applaud them nonetheless."

And in the darker recesses of our cosmos,
God mutters, *The uncertainty principle
has everything to do with people's faith.*

Eschaton

The crowd clamoring for revenge
The gods arranging an icy fire
The unclever birds picking sides
Blood on everyone's hands
Death on everyone's minds
In the village a quiet like amnesia
The king biting his tongue bitterly
The queen removing her crown
The people bristling with hunger
Night falling too quickly, blackly
Iron swords hanging from rafters
It's fate, someone said, *no going back*
It's karma, someone's sister added
People chanted *light the flames*
Stars shivered and fell in droves
Half the sky groaned, half swooned
Love said to itself *I'm an enigma*
And then everything grew still

An Accounting of His Life

Have you ever crossed a sea in a slow boat?
If so, you'll know how many idle hours
of his odyssey Ulysses spent staring vacantly

out at the horizon, or worrying a hangnail,
or marking crosshatches on his favorite sword
to number, weekly, his bowel movements.

Even as a child, Ulysses loved counting, so
recalled his mother, Anticlea, relating how
the boy used his limestone pebbles to tally

the # of squashed spiders on their stairwells;
the # of ticks on their pigs, the # of pigpens
in their barnyard stalls; also, the # of grids

on Ithaca's prison doors; the # of ladders
and rungs leading into their royal attics;
of fences and water wells scattered across

their fields, orchards, and island gardens.
Ulysses fondly remembered his youthful tallies
during his long Aegean crossing, when the sea

was as calm as the open eye of a pond and
his men drowsy and sated, dreaming their own
private visions of home. Some nights, Ulysses

counted the # of stars climbing the sky's black
trellises when the moon scythed merely a glint
of light, those stars numerous as his sighs.

Other nights, with his silver abacus, he'd reckon
the men's wages, savoring the musical clack-
clack of calculations as waves slapped the hull.

Sometimes he recounted the raw rope burns
he'd suffered enduring the sirens' serenades,
or he'd number the nymphs whom he'd bedded—

scores it seemed—with fragrantly oiled bodies,
with their lilting foreign voices. Then Penelope's
face would materialize like an icon before him,

and he'd # her virtues as if they were pearls,
she his prize bounty from Zeus' coffers. But,
more often, his voyage was too tumultuous for

reverie, Poseidon releasing his thunderous power
with storms so deafening and exhausting they'd
numb his senses, the waves crushing his ship

with huge mountains of water, his best sailors
howling like madmen, and his journey a hellish
siphoning of his years into a stupefying void.

When these storms finally ended, Ulysses fell
into a sleep as deep and mysterious as eternity,
and when he awoke, he'd begin, once again,

to # all that roused him: his wife, his son,
the branches he'd bent into his nuptial bed,
today's ration of dried fish awaiting his mouth.

Fontaine le Port

That autumn when I was five and you seven,
when we roamed the steep fields leading to the Seine,
me grasping handfuls of dry rushes, yellow as tobacco stains,
you saying *vite, vite*, in your newfound French,
before flopping down on the river's bank
to pull a slim blade of tasseled grass
into your mouth—

—seventy years ago, and our childhood's flown
airily into the past, just like those distant sunsets seeping into
their own light, huge mirrors swallowing the sky's dome;
oh, how we yearned to hold hostage everything
we touched, to halt every hour, to be so still
that the world became invisible
and indivisible from us—

How can it be, dear sister, that we ache
with such tenderness for what we've lost, knowing
that nothing returns without being altered irretrievably,
that being mortal means losing everything, even
a damp attic room in Maurice Chevalier's
summer *gîte*, where we built dreams
made of sandpaper?

I watch us wading again into that cold current,
unattended by our errant parents, two brave *jeune filles*
who believed time would never end because it didn't exist,
because we were free as the gilt fish slipping
past the river's weeds, free as the siskins
sifting clouds through their wings,
for death hadn't grazed us yet.

A Meditation

Under clouds white and frayed as old lace,
on a narrow tree branch in a Nilgiri forest,

I found a crested treeswift's nest ornamented
with bark, feathers, flower petals, and butterflies

pilfered mid-flight by those fork-tailed birds.
One blue-grey egg was laid there, glued to its nest

with swift spittle, surrounded by dead honey bees
like amber beads decorating the nest's perimeter.

The parent swifts were nowhere in sight, so I
worried about a brainfever bird or raven

ransacking the nest, then stealing or devouring
that single egg laid so lovingly in its bower.

I relived, on another forest outing, my tripping
over a banded krait, that "seven-step snake,"

with its neurotoxic venom. All around me, roots
erupted from the forest floor like cinnamon quills,

and a gentle cacophony of sounds, filtered through
ten million leaves, reminded me how alive I was

and how fraught—how every breath was laden
with the freight of being and nothingness,

as were that solitary swift egg, its sculpted nest,
the forest's deadly reptiles and poisonous webs—

every living thing cradling its beginning and end
in its genes. Awe filled me and I turned away.

Requiem

I.

How strange that one of her last paintings,
an enormous canvas, shows a mighty horse

tumbling out of the sky upside-down,
his massive legs pumping the air, his mouth

agape, nostrils flared, eyes rolled back
in terror. What did it mean? I never asked

my mother, because the painting's power
rendered me abashed and speechless.

It was as if she'd mysteriously divined
my most private nightmare.

II.

My mother claimed her eyes were hazel,
when, in truth, they were burnt umber—

my favorite pigment on her easel tray—
truer than sienna, warmer than amber,

less golden than ochre, bolder than russet,
more potent than sepia. She believed

her hair was black, but it was more lustrous
than obsidian, as thick as a filly's mane.

It hung in a long braid down her spine, so
when she walked, it swung its pendulum

in time to the rhythm of her stroll,
air whirlpooling invisibly behind her.

III.

Beautiful, my mother's feet—
long, slender, silky as a baby's skin.

Eighty-six-years-old and she's dying,
gasping from lungs ransacked by cancer,

her mind muddled by rogue cells and radiation.
I rub her perfect feet, so like Aphrodite's

with their elegant toes, their nacre nails
opalescent and smooth. But listening to her

ruptured breath, her agonal wheezing is
a torment to us both: she gasps, an air-

tossed fish, her gills pleading for oxygen
as her brave, sacred life flees from us.

IV.

Yet her shapely feet, her face and body,
grow more beautiful as death's dark horses

draw nearer, as morphine drips its dread
and amnesia into her veins. Now the horses

snort and paw the ground near her gurney,
their muzzles steaming; the charioteer snaps

his whip and stokes a whirlwind encircling
her room. A moment before her death,

my mother suddenly sits up wide-eyed,
memorizing my sister and my faces;

she opens her mouth to speak, but, instead,
inhales a huge draft of air, then lies down

and dies. A ripple of something—
her spirit? a mirage of consciousness?—

lifts from her skin, as her lovely feet curl
inward like seashells, her toenails bluing

as the wild-hooved horses drag her off
into their vast and endless plains.

Notes and Dedications

Hafiz (or Hafez, 1325-1390) was a Persian lyric poet who wrote devout, mystical verse, and who's widely considered to be Iran's greatest writer. October 12th is annually celebrated as Hafiz Day in Iran.

Omnicide (p. 2) was published as a broadside for the "Insectageddon Festival" on September 25, 2021, at the High Line Park in New York City. Chilean artist and poet, Cecilia Vicuña, directed the festival.

Desert Tortoise Lament (p. 3): Gabrielino-Tongva villages occupied the Los Angeles basin for thousands of years and were commonly located near the Los Angeles, San Gabriel, and Santa Ana Rivers. This poem's dedicated to Katherine Wells, friend, artist, New Mexican petroglyph conservationist at Mesa Prieta Petroglyph Project (MPPP), and a kind mentor to lost desert tortoises.

The scene in *Indonesian Corpse Flower* (p. 5) occurs at the Huntington Library and Botanical Gardens in San Marino, California.

February Reverie (p. 10) is for my grandson, Ethan Diaz, and my granddaughter, Laila Falk.

Transformations (p. 14) is for my younger daughter, Leah Rose Falk, a healer of bodies and souls.

Magic Bullets (p. 17) and *Rebuttal* (p. 19) were written in memory of my father, Robert Leopold Simon, a California composer, ethnomusicologist, and educator (1923-2013).

No Wars Are Won (p. 20) is dedicated, in memoriam, to decorated World War II war hero and my father-in-law, Martin Falk (1921-2011), to my husband, Robert Falk, and grandson Alex Flores Falk.

A Philosophical Argument (p. 21), *Spindrift* (p. 28), *Space Dot : A Love Letter* (p. 29), and *No Wars Are Won* (p. 20) were also written for Robert Falk.

Pain Logs #1, *#5*, and *#7* (pp. 24, 26, 27) are dedicated to my brilliant and life-sustaining pain management physician, Dr. Eric Cheeho Kim.

Pain Log #2 (p. 25) and *Fontaine le Port* (p. 74) are for my beloved sister and spectacular quilt maker, Tamara Ambroson—my lifelong sidekick, and an invaluable and insightful editor.

Regarding *Space Dot : A Love Letter* (p. 29), the etymology of the Old English word *leof* derives from the Proto-German, "leubaz," which means "dear" or "beloved."

What I Was Taught (p. 31) ends with lines drawn from the poem, *Planetarium*, by Adrienne Rich.

I first encountered this quotation by Niels Bohr (p. 35) during a conversation many years ago with poet Robert Mezey. He discovered it cited in one of John Berryman's *Dream Songs*.

In *Saturday Night Fever* (p. 36), *Sine amore, nihil est vita* is a Latin maxim which means "Without love, life is nothing," suggesting that life is pointless, or meaningless, without love.

A Theory of Eyebrows (p. 39): On December 2, 2015, Syed Rizwan Farook and Tashfeen Malik, a married couple living in Redlands, California, waged a terrorist attack upon the Inland Regional Center in San Bernardino, murdering 14 people and injuring 22. Hours later, police killed them in their car during a shootout.

The *Sheelah-Na-Gig* (p. 47) upon which this ekphrastic poem is based is located in a 12th c. church in the village of Kilpeck, Herefordshire, England. Like other Sheelahs found in England, Ireland, and Wales, this sandstone sculpture exhibits several defining features: a bald head, large eyes, a gaunt torso, and she squats, holding open her enlarged genitalia. There are many competing theories about the significance of these Celtic carvings, but it seems likely that Sheelah is a symbol of fertility.

Untold Lives of Ancient Greece (p. 51): Historical records indicate that Lasthenia (circa 4th c. BCE) was born in Mantinea, an ancient city in Arcadia, in the Peloponnese. A student of Plato's at the Academy, she was known for dressing as a man. After Plato's death, she continued her studies with his nephew, Speusippus, with whom she purportedly had an affair.

Gyn-Ecology (p. 53) takes its title from Mary Daly's groundbreaking book, *Gyn/Ecology: The Metaethics of Radical Feminism* (Beacon Press, 1980). This poem's dedicated to California poet Amy Gerstler, a "queen of metaphor," who writes wonderfully imaginative, playful, wise, and memorable poems.

The Blue Bridge (p. 60) and *Requiem* (p. 76) are dedicated to the memory of my mother, Los Angeles artist and sculptor, Baila Goldenthal (1925-2011).

Midsummer's Day (p. 62) is for wonderful poet and fellow traveler, Garrett Hongo, a gracious friend for forty years.

The Widow (p. 68) is for my dear friend, Peggy Shumaker, a superb poet, loyal colleague, and bringer of light into the world. This poem also honors the memory of her husband, Joe Usibelli (1938-2022).

A Meditation (p. 75): The Nilgiris (Blue Mountains) are a range that borders the states of Tamil Nadu, Karnataka, and Kerala in South India. Banded kraits are found throughout

India, and they're known as the "seven-step snake" in Tamil Nadu because their venom, which contains a mixture of neurotoxins, is often lethal within minutes. Banded kraits dwell in a variety of habitats, ranging from forests to agricultural lands, and they're endemic throughout Asia. This poem is for Karen Afner Gordon, staunch friend of my youth and beyond, who now meanders through the lush landscapes of Ecuador.

States of Being (p. 69) is for my older daughter, Naomi Falk, a brilliant criminal attorney and Los Angeles County Public Defender.

An Accounting of His Life (p. 72) is for the extraordinary poet, B.H. (Pete) Fairchild, my cherished friend for over thirty years and a near neighbor.

Perpetual thanks to the members of my writers' group—W.J. Herbert, Frances McConnel, Nancy Ware, and Cynthia Tuell—for their loyal support, editorial expertise, and friendship over decades.

My gratitude, as well, to poets Mihaela Moscaliuc and Michael Waters, who continue to be stalwart and much-loved friends. Their poetry has guided me through both dark and illuminating waters.

About Maurya Simon

Maurya Simon's *The Blue Bridge* is her twelfth volume of poems. *La Sirena: A Novella in Verse* (2024) was a National Book Award and Pulitzer Prize nominee. Simon's collection, *The Wilderness: New and Selected Poems*, received the 2019 Independent Booksellers Association's Gold Medal in Poetry. Simon's opera, "Tamar," based on her verse libretto, with music composed by French American composer, Eliane Aberdam, premiered at the University of Rhode Island. A Fulbright Senior Research Fellow (South India), NEA Poetry Fellow, and a Poetry Society's Lucille Medwick Memorial and Cecil Hemley Memorial Awardee, she's served residencies at the American Academy in Rome, the Baltic Centre for Writers & Translators (Visby, Sweden), Hawthornden Castle (Edinburgh, Scotland), the Djerassi Resident Artists Program (Santa Cruz, CA), and at the MacDowell Colony (Peterborough, NH). Simon's poems have been translated into Hebrew, French, Spanish, Romanian, Bengali, Greek, and Farsi. She serves as a Professor Emerita in the Creative Writing Department at the University of California, Riverside.

Books from Etruscan Press

Zarathustra Must Die | Dorian Alexander
The Disappearance of Seth | Kazim Ali
The Last Orgasm | Nin Andrews
Son of a Bird | Nin Andrews
Drift Ice | Jennifer Atkinson
Crow Man | Tom Bailey
Coronology | Claire Bateman
Viscera | Felice Belle
Reading the Signs and other itinerant essays | Stephen Benz
Topographies | Stephen Benz
What We Ask of Flesh | Remica L. Bingham
The Greatest Jewish-American Lover in Hungarian History | Michael Blumenthal
No Hurry | Michael Blumenthal
Choir of the Wells | Bruce Bond
Cinder | Bruce Bond
The Other Sky | Bruce Bond and Aron Wiesenfeld
Peal | Bruce Bond
Scar | Bruce Bond
Until We Talk | Darrell Bourque and Bill Gingles
Big Time | Rus Bradburd
Poems and Their Making: A Conversation | Moderated by Philip Brady
Crave: Sojourn of a Hungry Soul | Laurie Jean Cannady
Toucans in the Arctic | Scott Coffel
Sixteen | Auguste Corteau
Don't Mind Me | Brian Coughlan
Wattle & daub | Brian Coughlan
Body of a Dancer | Renée E. D'Aoust
Generations: Lullaby with Incendiary Device, The Nazi Patrol, and How It Is That We | Dante Di Stefano, William Heyen, and H. L. Hix
Ill Angels | Dante Di Stefano
Aard-vark to Axolotl: Pictures From my Grandfather's Dictionary | Karen Donovan
Trio: Planet Parable, Run: A Verse-History of Victoria Woodhull, and Endless Body | Karen Donovan, Diane Raptosh, and Daneen Wardrop
Scything Grace | Sean Thomas Dougherty
Areas of Fog | Will Dowd
The Red Branch | Myles Dungan
Romer | Robert Eastwood
Wait for God to Notice| Sari Fordham
Bon Courage: Essays on Inheritance, Citizenship, and a Creative Life| Ru Freeman
Surrendering Oz | Bonnie Friedman
Funeral Playlist | Sarah Gorham
Nahoonkara | Peter Grandbois
Triptych: The Three-Legged World, In Time, and Orpheus & Echo | Peter Grandbois, James McCorkle, and Robert Miltner

The Candle: Poems of Our 20th Century Holocausts | William Heyen
The Confessions of Doc Williams & Other Poems | William Heyen
The Football Corporations | William Heyen
A Poetics of Hiroshima | William Heyen
September 11, 2001: American Writers Respond | Edited by William Heyen
Shoah Train | William Heyen
American Anger: An Evidentiary | H. L. Hix
As Easy As Lying | H. L. Hix
As Much As, If Not More Than | H. L. Hix
Chromatic | H. L. Hix
Demonstrategy: Poetry, For and Against | H. L. Hix
First Fire, Then Birds | H. L. Hix
God Bless | H. L. Hix
I'm Here to Learn to Dream in Your Language | H. L. Hix
Incident Light | H. L. Hix
Legible Heavens | H. L. Hix
Lines of Inquiry | H. L. Hix
Rain Inscription | H. L. Hix
Shadows of Houses | H. L. Hix
Wild and Whirling Words: A Poetic Conversation | Moderated by H. L. Hix
All the Difference | Patricia Horvath
Art Into Life | Frederick R. Karl
Free Concert: New and Selected Poems | Milton Kessler
Who's Afraid of Helen of Troy: An Essay on Love | David Lazar
Black Metamorphoses | Shanta Lee
Sign & Breath: Voice & the Literary Tradition | Edited by Shanta Lee and Philip Brady
Mailer's Last Days: New and Selected Remembrances of a Life in Literature |
J. Michael Lennon
Parallel Lives | Michael Lind
The Burning House | Paul Lisicky
Museum of Stones | Lynn Lurie
Quick Kills | Lynn Lurie
Synergos | Roberto Manzano
The Gambler's Nephew | Jack Matthews
American Mother | Colum McCann with Diane Foley
The Subtle Bodies | James McCorkle
An Archaeology of Yearning | Bruce Mills
Arcadia Road: A Trilogy | Thorpe Moeckel
Venison | Thorpe Moeckel
So Late, So Soon | Carol Moldaw
The Widening | Carol Moldaw
Clay and Star: Selected Poems of Liliana Ursu | Translated by Mihaela Moscaliuc
Cannot Stay: Essays on Travel | Kevin Oderman
White Vespa | Kevin Oderman
Also Dark | Angelique Palmer
Fates: The Medea Notebooks, Starfish Wash-Up, and overflow of an unknown self |

Ann Pedone, Katherine Soniat, and D. M. Spitzer
The Dog Looks Happy Upside Down | Meg Pokrass
Mr. Either/Or | Aaron Poochigian
Mr. Either/Or: All the Rage| Aaron Poochigian
The Shyster's Daughter | Paula Priamos
Help Wanted: Female | Sara Pritchard
American Amnesiac | Diane Raptosh
Dear Z: The Zygote Epistles | Diane Raptosh
Human Directional | Diane Raptosh
I Eric America | Diane Raptosh
The Future of an Illusion | Rush Rankin
50 Miles | Sheryl St. Germain
Saint Joe's Passion | J.D. Schraffenberger
Lies Will Take You Somewhere | Sheila Schwartz
Fast Animal | Tim Seibles
One Turn Around the Sun | Tim Seibles
Voodoo Libretto: New and Selected Poems | Tim Seibles
With No Hat | Tim Seibles
Rough Ground | Alix Anne Shaw
A Heaven Wrought of Iron: Poems From the Odyssey | D. M. Spitzer
American Fugue | Alexis Stamatis
Variations in the Key of K | Alex Stein
The Casanova Chronicles | Myrna Stone
Luz Bones | Myrna Stone
In the Cemetery of the Orange Trees | Jeff Talarigo
The White Horse: A Colombian Journey | Diane Thiel
The Arsonist's Song Has Nothing to Do With Fire | Allison Titus
Bestiality of the Involved | Spring Ulmer
The Waw | Jacqueline Gay Walley
Silk Road | Daneen Wardrop
Sinnerman | Michael Waters
The Fugitive Self | John Wheatcroft
YOU. | Joseph P. Wood
Leaves Borrowed from Human Flesh | Abigail Ardelle Zammit

Etruscan Press Is Proud of Support Received From

Wilkes University

Ohio Arts Council

The Stephen & Jeryl Oristaglio Foundation

Community of Literary Magazines and Presses

National Endowment for the Arts

Drs. Barbara Brothers & Gratia Murphy Endowment

Founded in 2001 with a generous grant from the Oristaglio Foundation, Etruscan Press is a nonprofit cooperative of poets and writers working to produce and promote books that nurture the dialogue among genres, achieve a distinctive voice, and reshape the literary and cultural histories of which we are a part.

Etruscan Press
www.etruscanpress.org
Etruscan Press books may be ordered from

Consortium Book Sales and Distribution
800.283.3572
www.cbsd.com

Etruscan Press is a 501(c)(3) nonprofit organization.
Contributions to Etruscan Press are tax deductible
as allowed under applicable law.
For more information, a prospectus,
or to order one of our titles,
contact us at books@etruscanpress.org.

www.ingramcontent.com/pod-product-compliance
Lightning Source LLC
Jackson TN
JSHW061948190226
98286JS00005B/8
9798990767829